Have you ever struggled with self worth? Continued to repeat bad patterns in your life? *Paddling Upstream* is a true, raw and honest account of one woman's three-decade journey to discovering herself and finding her worth. Through a number of challenging relationships, unique adventures and trying to have a baby on her own, she realized everything she was searching for all along was always inside of her. An important book for both women and men, *Paddling Upstream* spotlights the connection between our self worth and the choices we make in love and life.

A JOURNEY TO SELF WORTH

PADDLING UPSTREAM

LAURI TUCKER

Copyright © 2019 by Lauri Tucker

All rights reserved.

No part of this book may be reproduced in any form or by any electronic or mechanical means, including information storage and retrieval systems, without written permission from the author, except for the use of brief quotations in a book review.

Design & Layout by StandoutBooks.com

ISBN: 978-0-9706726-8-1

Contents

Chapter 1: Sperm   1

Chapter 2: How can someone like you be single?   7

Chapter 3: The one that got away   13

Chapter 4: Breakups and breakdowns   29

Chapter 5: Finding myself   41

Chapter 6: Filling a void   55

Chapter 7: My fertility journey   59

Chapter 8: Picking myself up   71

Chapter 9: IVF   77

Chapter 10: Round two   91

Chapter 11: Why I chose to stop fertility treatments   97

Chapter 12: The climb to get my life back   105

CHAPTER 1

Sperm

Have you ever met someone who's spent $5,600 on sperm? Well, now you have. Yea. $5,600. On sperm. From four men I've never met. Lots of strangers' sperm. That adds up to approximately three to four tropical vacations I missed out on, where I probably could've been the lucky (or unlucky) recipient of free sperm from a drunk frat boy or pool boy on spring break.

As visions (nightmares) of sperm swim through my head and that dollar amount sinks in, along with the additional $8,000 or so that I spent on procedures, medicine and travel, I shake my head and half dry heave/half smile now that I've ended fertility treatments after 1.5 years of trying to have a baby on my own. I can now laugh almost as much as I've cried about the experience.

That journey was something I was sure would end up the way I wanted — me holding a baby at the end of it. After years of bad and unfulfilling relationships, there just wasn't anyone I felt like even seeing more than once a week, let alone living or procreating with. I've always done life really well on my own, so I knew having a baby on my own was the right step for me.

So that's what I tried to do when I was 42. I didn't think my age would be a deterrent, since I was healthy, super fit and all my hormones were operating just fine. None of that perimenopause or menopause bullshit was anywhere in sight, so I figured I would find the golden egg and become a mom with no problem.

But before I freak you out by talking about intrauterine insemination (IUI), aging ovaries and donor sperm, I figure I better explain how I ended up here. And by here, I mean the place where I accepted and loved myself enough to know I could pave my own path, one that was different from what society said I was supposed to be on; how my journey to self worth led me to knowing I was ready and capable of bringing a child into the world in a non-traditional way.

I was pretty independent and opinionated throughout my childhood, so the fact that I've ventured off the beaten path isn't that big of a surprise. I've honestly always felt that my path would be different. But when I was a child, my dreams were like a lot of other kids. I wanted to marry Michael Jackson (long before I knew he wasn't really into women), be famous and be a kindergarten teacher. I also remember wanting to have kids young, like in my early 20s, like my mom did. But that is not *quite* how things turned out. I'm pretty sure having a child by donor sperm as a single woman at age 42 wasn't one of my dreams back then or one of the story plots I read about in my elementary school reading class.

While I'm glad I didn't end up being an octomom by age 24, I always thought I'd probably have at least ONE child before I was 40. But as time went on, I never really had the dire urge to hurry up and have kids. I was just busy living my life, having fun, dating terrible men who sucked the life out of me and ruined the fairy tale — you know, stuff like that. At times I have thought that maybe I just didn't have a biological clock like everyone else, or maybe I wasn't meant to have kids and that I'd maybe just remain the fun aunt, or at some point perhaps I'd decide to do it on my own if I didn't meet anyone. But then out of the blue, at 42, the clock came a tickin' — and let me tell ya, it was deafening.

My journey, like everyone else navigating life, has been nothing less than a roller coaster. Sad, happy, rough, depressing, exciting, adventurous. I guess as humans, we're meant to experience all of these things. And I know now that everything I've been through had to happen so I could wake up and accept the path I've always been meant to follow. I needed to realize I was resilient, strong and capable of doing anything

I put my mind to, including living my true, authentic self without caring what others think of my choices.

So why Paddling Upstream? Doesn't that seem like something one should avoid? I used to think so. But I discovered at age 40, after five years of really focusing on being my true self, notably as a single woman, I was the happiest I'd ever been. I started really thinking about what led me to such a great place.

A lot of shit, that's what.

But honestly, it's the shit that's made me a stronger person, and made me who I am. The shit also gave me strength to get through hard times during the 1.5 years of trying to have a baby and honestly, anything else that comes my way. Just like paddling upstream is a struggle, so is navigating all the avenues of life: relationships, jobs, health and more. But when you're able to fight through the current and reach your destination, you realize how resilient you've really been all along. Cheesy? Yea. But true.

I've always said that being happy is a choice. And don't get me wrong, sometimes it's hard to continuously make that choice. It's really easy to fall into the negative mindset when things don't go the way you expected them to go. The world is full of negative things, which if you let them, can really fuck up your well being. And I've had plenty of fucked up moments. But if you really use your time to be truly present and look for the lessons and growth opportunities in each moment and each experience, and not continuously look back or too far forward, your life can be extremely fulfilling and maybe even an inspiration to others. If we can accept that all things happen in order to keep us on our path, or show us the path, it makes it a lot easier to keep moving forward.

I'm in the communications field professionally, and personally I've always used writing as an outlet, so writing a book about my journey so far and what I've learned from it all just made sense. Maybe my motivation for writing this book is so I can look back when I'm 90 and reminisce (or hell, remember what I did), or maybe it's so relatives (who are alive long after I pass) can look back and see that someone they're related to really lived a great life by taking the road less traveled. Perhaps I wanted to let other women, and men, know that you don't have to depend on someone else for your happiness. Or maybe it's so the child that I may still have someday will know how much I wanted them and was willing to do to be a mom (and so they know how cool their mom was). I don't know if anyone will read this, but one good thing about being happy and 40-something is that you really don't give a shit if anyone doesn't. But if you are holding this book right now, thank you.

PADDLING UPSTREAM

When you were a child, what did you want to be when you grew up?

_____
_____
_____
_____

Are you honoring your inner child now? If so, how? If not, why?

_____
_____
_____
_____

What can you do to work toward those goals again?

_____
_____
_____
_____

CHAPTER 2

How can someone like you be single?

I've tried for years to come up with a good comeback to that question. I've told people everything from "I have a lot of back hair" to "I turn into a monster at midnight," but for some reason my answers don't really seem to convince them. I know people mean that question as some sort of weird compliment, but after hearing it 1,000 times, the only thing I can muster is a giant sigh (although the voice inside my head usually can muster "Fuck Off!").

But seriously, why am I single? The big secret? I've chosen it. I really just cannot put up with bullshit anymore. But I used to. A lot. For years. Some of the things I've run into — and away from — include:

1. Domestic abuse (emotional, verbal and physical)
2. Cheaters

3. Compulsive liars
4. Married men who don't tell me they're married until date 20, or surprise me on date one, which is an extra special good time.
5. Men in their 40s, without jobs, who have four kids and live with their mothers, but lie about where they live and work
6. Gambling addicts
7. Substance abusers
8. Men that swear they're over the ex's, start dating me, only to disappear out of the blue, leaving me to just "guess" they got back together with their ex. Usually I'm right because they pop back up to "apologize" and ask me out again usually within a year.
9. Sociopaths and narcissistic men who want me to be their girlfriend/wife after one date, then proceed to send me 756 texts a day and get mad and pout (and find other women who will pay attention) when I don't respond to each and every one of them.
10. Men going through divorces that "swear" they're ready for a relationship. Only for me to realize that they just don't know how to stand on their own two feet and they want a mama, not a girlfriend. No man babies!

11. Smothering men who can't spend one minute alone and base their entire happiness on you. These are the worst by the way.

I'm guessing you might get the picture and understand why I've chosen to be single. This is just a small snapshot of some of the men I've dated in the past 20 years. The funny thing is, No. 11 was also me in my 20s and part of my 30s. I was the smothering one and I found other smothering people, or rather, codependent people, to date. I realize now it's because I had no self worth. All the men in this list all had one thing in common: they were all somewhat broken, and I, subconsciously, was attracting that because I was also broken and needed someone to fix. I really needed to fix myself, but I didn't realize that back then.

I used to ignore red flags, so I take some responsibility for making bad choices. But some of these things, like the lying and abuse, happened after the relationship had been established for awhile. Textbook. I was a lot younger and didn't have any idea who I was and what I wanted. I used to be easily manipulated when I was younger, and my goodness was taken advantage of often. I was too giving. Too trusting. I gave all of my heart, my love, my time, and sometimes my money, before anyone even proved they were worth it. I ignored the red flags and was attracted to damaged men like a moth to a flame.

But one thing all of these bad relationships ultimately gave me was one important lesson: TRUST YOUR INTUITION. If something feels off, it probably is. If there's one thing I've gained, it's an intuition that is stronger than stink on a skunk. I consider myself lucky, as I always "woke up" just in time with these guys. No matter how long those awful relationships dragged on, I was always smart enough to leave and end things before I married any of them. And over the years I just got smarter and really honed my red flag o'meter, aka my gut feeling,

But of course the good one I thought I should've married, I didn't.

What are some of your challenging dating experiences?

Are you in a challenging dating experience, or marriage, now? Do you have red flags and if so, what are they?

Why do you stay, or why did you leave?

Do you want to be single? Or does being single scare you? Why or why not?

CHAPTER 3

The one that got away

I was in an abusive relationship from 1995-1998 with a guy I worked with (who I'll call Brad) and who left his wife while she was pregnant with their second child. PREGNANT! Because he was so "miserable" — his words. I feel so gross even admitting out loud now, 24 years later, that I dated him. But I think I'm ready to really talk about it. (Don't worry, he's not the one that got away.)

I was 20 at the time, and lost. My parents had just gone through a horrible divorce that started when I was 19, and my father wasn't in my life very often when I really needed him, and basically I was an idiot and let an older man I met at work manipulate me — and abuse me, emotionally, verbally and physically.

It was a textbook abusive relationship. Brad was seven years older than me and very handsome. He turned heads everywhere he went as a Brad Pitt looka-like. I met him at work, and we were friends first. As I got to know him more, as I mentioned above, he told me and others how miserable his marriage was. And I fell for it. I honestly don't remember now, 24 years later, how we even started dating and how we ended up living together, with me helping to take care of his newborn baby. NEWBORN. I was 20 taking care of a man's newborn baby. Typing that right now makes me physically ill and makes me want to slap my 20-year-old self. What the actual hell was I thinking? I wasn't. I was obviously looking for attention, from anyone, and simply, love.

Within six months, Brad started putting down my appearance — an appearance he of course was initially attracted to — and the way I dressed, often telling me I looked "too slutty" and that I was always trying to get attention. He convinced me to cut my long blonde hair, color it to a very mousy brown so I looked more plain and unavailable (his words), and also convinced me to dress differently. Sort of like a nun or pilgrim. I remember he often would call me fat at a size 6 and tell me I had fat milky thighs when we were in the middle of a fight. To this day, those words still stick in my head. I clearly remember one of the worst moments with him, when his two children were sleeping in the next room in one of our apartments. I had gone out with a few of my girlfriends for the evening. When I got home, he accused me of "probably flirting" with too many guys based on the way I was dressed. He started getting up in my face as I was trying to get my pajamas on and just go to bed. He grabbed me and as I pushed him to get away and jumped across the bed to get away from him, he kicked me in the back and I went flying into the stereo system that was up against the wall. I remember running outside in my underwear and a tank top trying to get away from him. He came outside running after me, begging me to get back inside so I didn't make a scene. I ran back inside and called 911. He then started crying on his knees in front of me, begging me to hang up because his kids were in the house. And of course, I did. 911 called back; he was about an inch from my face and whispered that I'd "better say the call was a mistake," and again, I did. I told them one of the kids accidentally dialed them. They asked me repeatedly if I was OK. I said yes. I was scared. To death.

Another time we were in my car arguing in a parking lot. About what I have no idea, but I remember it being cold and dreary and I can still picture myself right now clear as day in that car. I remember him out of the blue taking his fist and slamming it down onto my right thigh full force as I started driving out of the lot. I remember screaming in pain and in shock about what had just happened. When I got to his mother's house, I told her, hoping I'd get some help, but she blamed me for "making" him hit me. Then it all finally made sense. That's how he was raised.

There were so many more awful moments in those 2.5 years, which included having food thrown at me during an argument and him coming in between me and my best friend, Marcia, causing us to end our friendship after seven years of going to school together and being roommates. It's something I regret. But I am happy to say she and I recovered from that six months later and are still friends to this day. I think I've blocked the rest of the moments out because I don't remember everything during those years. I mostly just remember those years being really dark, from my parents split, trying to get on my feet and dating that asshole. It's hard for me to relive these violent memories, but also very healing, knowing how much I've grown and thrived after those bad experiences.

If you haven't been in an abusive relationship, it's hard to explain why you stay or why you put up with it. Honestly, it's because it tears your self esteem down to nothing. I would leave, and then go back — several times. It became a cycle of fights and forgiveness, and the hope that it would change. But it never did. It never does. Family members tried to intervene; my amazing aunt Vickie even let me move in with her in hopes that I'd never go back, but I did go back. Family eventually gave up, because I'm sure in their minds, if I went back, it couldn't be *that* bad, right?

It's hard for me to talk about because I am no longer that person who can be manipulated or abused. I cry as I write this because I can't even imagine being with such a pathetic excuse for a man now or allowing myself to be treated like that. I look back and want to hug the 20-year-old me who just needed some guidance, who just needed to understand her worth. To tell her she IS amazing, she IS capable, she IS worthy. That her life isn't dependent on a relationship or a man. That she can stand on her own two feet and succeed.

But the good news is, I did finally leave.

In the fall of 1998, when I was 23, aunt Vickie, who has always been like a second mother to me and desperately wanted me to get away from Mr. Abuser and open my life up to something more, asked me to go on vacation to Key West. I almost didn't go, because that would mean that I would be pissing off Brad. I ended up going anyway, against his wishes; I was filled with excitement, as this was my first time to a tropical paradise. I think he knew that once I got away from him and experienced life, I would never come back. He was right.

After a couple days enjoying the beach, my aunt and I decided to go parasailing one day, and as we walked up to the boat, I realized there was a really cute guy on the boat who looked my age. Matt was his name, and he worked for the parasailing company. As we sailed out to sea, we chatted and laughed, and I was captivated. I felt pretty for the first time in a long time. At the end of the trip I felt sad walking away, but, as I left the boat, he asked me if I wanted to go out later that night, to which I way-too excitedly replied, "Sure!" So my aunt and I walked away, me on cloud nine, her chuckling.

But as we walked away, I realized I hadn't given him my contact information, so my aunt told me to hurry and run back to the boat. As I was running back praying he hadn't sailed away, he came running around the corner looking for *me*. We bumped into each other and laughed with relief. Sounds like a movie right? Even now, 17 years later, I can honestly say it was love at first sight.

He met me and my aunt (to be safe) for dinner that night. After she retreated back to the hotel room, Matt and I spent the entire night drinking and dancing and falling in love. Crazy? Yes, but he was and still is that one person in my life that made me believe it can really happen that way. That once-in-a-lifetime, throw caution to the wind, young love that only comes around once in a lifetime. He was the fairy tale I had always believed as a child.

As I left the Keys to return to Ohio, I knew right then and there I had to move out and away from my abusive boyfriend. I did tell Matt about my situation when I met him, and when I got home, he called me every day to make sure I was safe, and that I was sticking to my plan of getting out. I literally had gone home and devised a plan to pack my stuff (I left any furniture I owned and just took what I could, including my cat) and move out while Brad was at work. After moving in with my amazing friend Chad (who I'm very grateful for to this day and am still close friends with), I got financially stable by working two to three jobs and eventually got my own place. Brad attempted to reach me a few times over the next few months but I threatened to press charges if he didn't leave me alone. He finally did, and I felt free.

A month later, Matt flew me to Vermont to meet his father, a trip I'll never forget, and he flew the next month to Columbus to meet my family for Thanksgiving. Because of the hurricane that hit Florida that fall, Matt had to move back to Vermont for awhile. His plan for the winter was to move out to Jackson Hole, Wyoming, where he had worked as a lifeguard at the indoor rec center the past few years so he could snowboard and hunt all winter.

I flew out to Jackson Hole five times that winter. You heard me right. Five times. And it was amazing.

Two 23-year olds splitting plane tickets and giant cell phone bills, back in the day when phone bills were as giant as the phones, was rough. But we did it because we just couldn't stay away from each other. We talked on the phone constantly and wrote and mailed numerous letters and cards (you know, in the "olden" days before email). I still have every single letter and card he wrote and sent to me. I've never been able to bring myself to throw it away. You know where this is going right?

So after a year of long-distance dating, and having my heart ripped out every time we parted, I started questioning when we would ever truly be together in the same place. Matt didn't want to move to Columbus because he needed open land and freedom and didn't want to live in the city. I was getting restless and also starting to want more for myself in general. More than working two or three jobs and having a boyfriend who lived 2,000 miles away. As I pondered life and my future at age 24, a random opportunity had come up where I had the chance to move to Nashville, Tennessee, of all things, to pursue a singing career. I know, it seems like it's out of left field, right? Let me explain.

In 1999, I had taken a trip to visit my best friend, Marcia, who had just moved to Nashville to continue the radio career she had started in Ohio when we were both 19. At 19, we were young and loving life and got to enjoy all the perks that came with the radio business, including backstage passes, traveling and meeting endless famous singers and bands, which led to us falling in love with country music, the limelight and the entertainment business. Those days were some of the best of my life. So how did the singing career come into play? Well, what's funny, I was never really a good singer, but after being exposed to the limelight all those years, I wanted to sing so bad!! So, since the last time I sang was at my 5th grade Christmas recital, I started taking singing lessons when I was 20, always with the crazy dream of being discovered. Well, fast forward four years later, when I was visiting Marcia in Nashville, I jumped on stage at a very popular downtown karaoke showbar, and the next thing I knew, the manager was offering me a job as the entertainment director. It was crazy. Not only could I be in the same city as my best friend again, I felt that it was maybe this was my big break! I had always dreamed of living in Nashville and now I had my chance with a good stable job and a social network already in place. Perfect!

But what I quickly realized is that everywhere you go, there you are. Once you start working in your "dream" town, you're working, and not really doing the things you love to do when you're on vacation.

While it was an amazing time in my life, I also quickly lost my way. I ended up getting an office job during the day to make ends meet and so I could have benefits, as singing in a nightclub wasn't cutting it. I also started bartending in an underground rave club that was super sketchy. I met some pretty sleazy guys in the entertainment business, got sucked into the partying lifestyle pretty heavily, and I even signed a development deal with a record label that ultimately went nowhere; I even had to threaten to sue them to let me out of the contract. After that ended, I started losing my interest in singing in Nashville, had eventually stopped singing all together, was exhausted from the fake people and partying lifestyle, and was tired of being broke as hell. I decided to move home to Columbus, Ohio in 2001 at the age of 26. I decided the best thing for me to do was to get a stable job, start college and put a band together there so I could get my life back on track and still fill the need I had to do something different.

OK, so back to Matt. You're probably wondering why I moved to Nashville and not Wyoming to be with him if I loved him as much as I said I did. Honestly, I didn't want to move to Wyoming because there wasn't any sort of work or career for me there, and it was so far away from my family, my home. Why was I the one who had to move to the middle of nowhere?

What would I even do? Serve beer to the men who just got done hunting out on the range? Run a brothel? There were no solid career opportunities for me in the places he wanted to live because they were so remote. And Matt didn't want to move to Columbus or Nashville because he needed open land and freedom and didn't want to live in the city.

So long story short, when I arrived in Nashville in 1999, I was thinking he would want to live there since there were mountains and open land, but he didn't. He said he needed to "visit" first to see if it's somewhere he'd want to be. Wait. What? All I was thinking was that I was there, wasn't that enough for him? I was so angry he wouldn't move for me, yet he was willing to roam around the country, state to state, for other things, so I ended it. Just like that. So quick. I was angry that he would move to other states to chase random jobs (he was really just enjoying his life and being 24), but he wouldn't move for US. I still remember where I was sitting in my room in Nashville, our conversation, how stunned he was that I was just ending it so easily. I just couldn't keep doing cross-country dating, with no end in sight, breaking down and sobbing every time we had to part. I just decided to put myself out of my misery. But little did I know our story would continue for 10 more years.

Matt and I happened to email each other at the same time four years later in 2003, wondering how each other were doing after all these years. He had moved again, and I had just broken up with someone I had dated during those four years after I had broken up with him. Turns out he was going to be near Columbus for work training, so we excitedly agreed to meet. I was extremely nervous, but when I saw him, all those old feelings came back. I still loved him, and he still loved me. We spent some time together but once again, had to go separate ways. Matt was living in South Dakota at the time, and neither one of us, again, were able to move to be together. So we once again parted ways and didn't talk again for about a year.

A year later, Matt reached out to me because he was again coming through town due to work. This time I was really excited to reconnect, as I thought of him a lot and missed him dearly. I felt like maybe this was really it, we were finally going to figure out a way to be together. But this time it was different. When I saw him, unexpectedly, I felt that something had changed — within me.

He visited me at my new condo in Columbus, and I could tell he felt out of place and not in his world. I was in a band at the time and going to college and was really loving traveling and being out and about in Columbus. I had become a different person; I had changed. I was in my own world, in my own place, trying to find myself and loving and experiencing life — something he was doing five years prior, when we first met when we were 23.

I remember sitting on the couch with him drinking wine, knowing we both felt it was the end. I also remember him saying that I looked happy, and he felt I was where I needed to be, and if he couldn't convince me to leave and move with him after all this time, he felt it was never going to happen. So, he left.

I watched him drive away, his taillights fading as he turned the corner, and I cried. I felt like someone died. I felt a grief I'd never felt before. He was here, in front of me, after all these years, and I let him just walk out the door. The man I had loved through my entire 20s was really gone this time, for good. I reached out to Matt one more time around 2010, when I was 35, realizing after all this time I had made a huge mistake letting him walk out the door all those years ago. He returned my email, happy to hear from me. But he also told me that after all this time, he had assumed I had moved on and probably had gotten married, so he felt once and for all he had to move on, too. Turns out he had gotten married a couple years prior and had a child — he couldn't believe I hadn't gotten married. After I sat and cried for awhile, and we exchanged a few emails reminiscing about old times, and how much we really loved each other back then, we agreed that continuing to email was extremely painful — too painful — and wasn't appropriate or respectful to his marriage.

The funny thing is, Matt always used to say that his biggest fear was that one day he'd call or email me, only to find out that I had gotten married. Turns out his fear became *my* reality. One of the last things he said in his email is that every time he hears the Adele song, Someone Like You, or drives through Ohio, he thinks of me, and it's wonderful and painful all at the same time to think about how much we loved each other and all the great times we had. Funny thing is, he lives in Upstate Michigan now, so close to me in Ohio, after all those years of living across the country from me.

I often think about how different my life would've been if I would've moved for Matt all those years ago when I was 24. We would've had a great love story, but I also wouldn't have lived and sang in Nashville, I wouldn't have gone to college here in Columbus, I wouldn't have all the memories from the band I was in and from the time I've spent with family and friends, and most of all, I never would've figured out who I was on my own, deep down to the core, without someone else defining me.

THE ONE THAT GOT AWAY

I still think of Matt, and still shed tears from time to time. He is my "one that got away." And he's the one that ultimately saved me, when I wasn't yet wise enough to save myself, from a previous abusive situation. I think the universe put him in my path to save me from the horrible situation I had been in previously. We loved hard, and loved the good and the bad about each other. But, through all the sadness of that, I'm thankful for that pure, honest real love he gave me. Love like that is only experienced once in a lifetime, and while we didn't end up together, I consider myself lucky to have felt it.

Did you have one that got away? If so, describe him/her.

Do you wish you would've stayed with that person? Why or why not?

How would your life be different if you would have stayed, or left?

CHAPTER 4

Breakups and Breakdowns

So let me explain what happened after I moved home from Nashville in 2001, when I was 26, after realizing I was not going to be the next Shania Twain. Luckily a former boss of mine in Columbus heard through the grapevine that I was moving home, and she offered me a job at the university where she worked. What a godsend. I immediately started working as a registrar for the graduate law programs. I loved it. And not only did I work there, it gave me the opportunity to get my degree there at a discount. It had aligned perfectly.

Unfortunately I had made the decision to bring my compulsive lying boyfriend (who I'll call Sam) of one year with me after he convinced me that he couldn't live without me and wanted to change his life. We moved in with my dad for a year so we could get on our feet, and then got our own apartment the following year. During that time when I was 26-28 years old, while there were some fun times, there were a lot of bad times, too. Sam would often go to work, turn his cell phone off and not show up back at home until 2 a.m. I'm pretty sure there were other girls involved; I know for a fact lots of alcohol and lots of lies. I ended up with panic attacks, low self esteem (again) and realizing again this is not what I wanted for my future. After almost four years of enduring that, I ended that relationship, moved out and bought my own condo at the age of 28. And for once, I wasn't dating anyone.

What finally gave me the courage? Honestly I don't know. I think there was just something in my gut that told me there had to be something more. This could NOT be my life. I was starting to gain self worth from going to college; I was growing and rising above him and that relationship. And again, I still had that feeling that I was meant for more. I think now, as I look back, this was when I first started realizing that maybe I was worth more than I was getting in return.

Initially I felt lonely in my condo, but I was coming into my own. I was working full time at the college I was attending full time (I went to school for five years, year round, while working full-time and graduated with a 3.89 GPA — one of my life's best accomplishments) and singing in a band around Columbus. All of this kept me really busy and my life began to be really fun again. Yea, I dated, casually, but mostly I just had a lot of fun with my friends, traveled and sang in a few bands over the next four years. But of course I ended up meeting someone in one of those bands, the one who would ultimately make me finally say, NO MORE.

When I was 32, I met a musician (who I'll call Ike) who had a TON of charisma. We ended up putting a band together. And since I always followed my heart and not my head, I fell for this guy who again, was going through a divorce. And again, he had two kids I fell in love with (who even lived in my condo for a brief period) and was a master manipulator. Ike was also a total pothead and other than being in the band, he didn't have a job. Sounds appealing, I know. He lived an hour away in the country, and every weekend I would pack up my stuff and drive out there, and abandon my own life with friends and family. There I was again, sacrificing my life for a man. I made excuses for him when people asked me about him. "Oh he's a stay-at-home dad and such a great father, that's why he's in a band, so he can stay home with his kids." When really, he was lazy AS FUCK, wanted to smoke weed all the time and didn't want to work. He told me once, "I don't know why you're with me, you're this amazing woman I am not good enough for you; I have nothing to offer you." But my dumb ass was like "oh but I love youuuuuu, and you just don't see your potential."

OMG right??!? Pathetic! I wish that one of my friends would've just slapped me really hard back then. One thing I've realized throughout my life is that men tell you <u>exactly</u> who they are, what they want and what they feel, but women hear what they want to hear and try to "fix."

The thing is, I know now he was right, he <u>wasn't</u> good enough for me and had nothing to offer me. And I should have walked away. But I didn't and just fell deeper in love with him because we had crazy chemistry that I couldn't walk away from. It almost felt like an addiction and I knew it wasn't good for me.

But two years later, when I was 34, it all came crashing down. We were madly in love at the time and had talked all along about getting married and having a child. Two years into the relationship he informed me over bacon and eggs on a Sunday that he changed his mind about having another child and that his two kids should be enough for me. I don't quite remember what happened at that point, as I think I blacked out.

That was the moment I finally "woke up." That was the virtual slap I needed. It's like I had been in a dream state for two years. He thought I was really going to be OK with his decision and just stay with him because I was sooooo in love, but even to my surprise, I ended it. I had come to the realization that I had lost myself. Completely. Ike had formed me into something he wanted. Just like the abuser, Brad, but with different tactics. I was defined by his life. I didn't know who I was anymore.

But had I ever?

After I ended the relationship with Ike, I hit rock bottom. I had never felt more lost in my life. I had finally felt like I had found the right one, after all my searching ... and there I was, alone again, feeling like a fool once again.

After being completely pathetic for a while, sobbing, drinking and being a victim, I decided to get myself into counseling once and for all and work through the reasons I kept making bad choices and ended up in dead-end relationships. And to be honest, I discovered a lot of it goes back to my father and my parents divorce when I was a teen. My dad was going through his own struggles and wasn't very present in my life at that point and his job required him to work very long hours, so I didn't really have the type of male guidance that I personally needed in my most formative years as a teen and into my 20s.

Now with that being said, our parents are real people; they aren't perfect and they struggle too, especially from having challenging childhoods themselves. I also realize that a lot of men of that generation weren't taught to share their feelings, or talk to their daughters about emotional topics, rather, they were taught to go to work and provide for the family. My dad had a hard childhood and also served as a Marine in Vietnam when he was just 17, which understandably he doesn't talk about and I'm sure no doubt challenges him every day of his life. One thing I do know is that he loves me (and I love him) and would never intentionally do anything to hurt me. I wish one day that he will open up to me and tell me about his life before I was born, so maybe I can understand him a little bit more, and feel closer to him emotionally. I want that more than anything. I think he and I could both benefit and heal in many ways from doing that.

It's crazy how our relationships and experiences with our parents and their struggles can really shape our future relationships. This is especially important between fathers and daughters. If a girl isn't getting attention, guidance and support from her father, she will often seek it somewhere else, often from men who don't have her best wishes or interests in mind. Which is exactly what I had done with all the men I dated. I often had sex way too soon with men I started dating and definitely had sex way too young as a teen in high school, and not just because of raging teen hormones (even though that shit is no joke!) and realize now it was because I was just searching for attention, and simply, connection.

Now with this being said, I want to make sure to state that there's nothing wrong with sex. As a woman, I own and feel comfortable with my sexuality. I just wish, back then, notably as a teen, I would've been a bit more secure with myself where sex wasn't a tool for love and attention — but hindsight is 20/20, right? We are dumb as teenagers; I didn't realize back then I was doing that, but I do now and happy to say it's no longer something I do.

Counseling during the breakup with Ike helped me get back my self-esteem that had taken a beating for 14 years and helped me to see that all along I had just been repeating what was familiar, which in a weird way, was "safe." I was trying to "fix" those who were broken but in my crazy eyes had "potential." Counseling taught me to listen to my gut feeling and pay attention to the red flags I had ignored so many times in the past. I also learned to love and forgive myself. And, it taught me to stop trying to FIX broken people. Broken people have to fix themselves. PERIOD.

But most of all, this is when I finally stopped basing my happiness on a person. Happiness, no matter how cliche it sounds, comes from inside of us. No one is responsible for or capable of giving you YOUR complete happiness. Even though it felt unbearable at the time, walking away from that relationship with Ike when I was 34 was one of the best things I did for my life. Why? Because if not, I would've ended up extremely unhappy and divorced within a couple years. And I wouldn't have started on the path to loving myself. And because for the first time in my life, I figured out who I was and how to be happy WITHOUT a man. From the time I was a teenager and until I was 34, I was a serial monogamist. I always had to be with someone. One relationship ended, one began, without a second thought. And now, while I've dated off and on, I've pretty much been single for eight years. The past eight years have been a choice.

And for eight years, I've been happier single than I ever was in a relationship and living an incredible life. Lots of adventure and travel, spending time with family and friends, taking care of myself through fitness and nutrition, working hard at my job, and laughing — a lot. Putting myself first — instead of a man — for the first time in my life. I found the way to create my own happiness.

Do I still run into bad apples? Yes. Do I still struggle with following my heart over my head sometimes? Sure. But am I more aware and secure? Yes. I found my strength. I finally discovered who I am. And most of all, I discovered my worth.

Ike called me when I was 42, eight years after I ended things, to apologize. Something I had always wanted to hear but didn't think I'd ever get. I cried through the hour-long call, realizing I had never gotten closure. He told me that because of me, he went back to college to get his degree and now had a marketing job and was very successful. He said I — and me leaving him — had made him want to be a better man. I had also heard through the grapevine prior to that call that he had gotten back together with the wife he had been divorcing back then, and they ended up having a third child. Remember, I ended things with him because he said he didn't want any more kids? I mentioned that and he said, "That was supposed to be with you" and went on to say he had always wanted a child with me but he had guilt over his divorce and putting his kids through that. He then went on to imply that he wasn't happy — once again with his current situation.

Unbelievable right? I stopped him right there and explained that I was no longer the girl he dated all those years ago, and that I was not going to listen to him complain, again, about his wife and his choices. I wished him well and ended the call. The next night, he called me again and I just ignored it. I knew he was trying to find his way back into my life. But that apology was closure for me and I haven't heard from him since. I was so proud I ignored that second incoming call — I had finally chosen myself.

Have you ever lost yourself in a relationship? If so, how?

What sacrifices did you make?

What lessons did you learn throughout
the relationship, or when it ended?

Do you still struggle with putting yourself and your needs first? If so, how can you start taking better care of yourself?

CHAPTER 5

Finding Myself

I always knew I was different. But I didn't know why. It was just something I felt when I was younger, deep in my gut. Right after high school, after discovering that my boyfriend of two years had just cheated on me with a friend, I remember a strong feeling like I was meant for something more; something more than what society says to do: go to college, get married, have 2.5 kids and a white picket fence. Not that there's anything wrong with that, but I think I even knew back then, subconsciously, that my story wouldn't end up like that.

What's crazy to me now, is that as a girl in her 20s, I remember having a feeling that I was going to end up alone. Now by "alone," I don't mean sad and crying-in-my-oatmeal alone, but alone in that I would walk this life as a single woman. It's hard to explain it now, but looking back there was always that intuition — one might argue premonition — that marriage and the fairy tale just weren't going to happen for me.

Mid-30s

After I picked myself up from ending the relationship with Ike from the last chapter, I started taking more risks as I focused on living my life solo. I was traveling more and seeking out adventure. I know now, just like when I moved to Nashville, I was desperately trying to find myself. Who was I? I set out on a mission to find out.

After developing a passion for whitewater rafting in my late 20s, and meeting some really fun, adventurous people who quit their jobs to live a life on the river during those trips, I signed up to learn how to raft guide on the New River in West Virginia in my late 30s. I can't even believe I did that now, as most of the people in the training class were broke and 20. And here I was, taking two weeks off from my Corporate America job, because I was emotionally (internally) a hot mess and was having a mid-30s crisis. Now that I look back, I think everyone on that river was searching for something, too. I thought I'd be wicked good guiding, too, because I was athletic and a great paddler after all. But let's just say that paddling as a guest in a raft with a guide telling you what to do, and actually leading and guiding a raft full of people down a raging river don't exactly go hand in hand. Let's be honest, I royally sucked at guiding a raft down Class

V whitewater (Class III too). I ended up getting hurt during my "checkout" run that would've allowed me to "graduate" and move on taking customers down the river all by my lonesome. After I got hurt, I felt that it was time to hang up my guiding dreams. The training was one of the hardest things I've ever done, and for the first time I had failed at a goal. That experience showed me I still did not have a strong sense of self or self worth. I still didn't know who I was to the core, and I didn't believe in myself. I still had a lot of work to do.

During that time, I had taken on a pretty intense fitness lifestyle and had also joined an outdoor club in Columbus and took whitewater kayaking lessons. I met some nice people and even started rock climbing, camping and hiking more, and found an even greater love for the outdoors. It was exciting and adventurous! I even learned to surf in Hawaii. Those times to this day have provided some of my favorite memories and the best years of my life. But most of all, it's the time when I started to find a greater love for myself. I started noticing that I was saying "no" more, I had more of an opinion, I wasn't wasting years in relationships with men who didn't deserve me, and most of all, I was taking risks and was happy. I was off the beaten path. I was also single. I now know that by wandering through the woods, climbing up large rocks and rafting through rapids — I found myself. Apparently I had to risk death a few times to realize my worth. But hey, it worked.

Rock Climbing in Red River Gorge, KY, in December 2011.

Hiking in Boulder, CO, May 2014

FINDING MYSELF

Rappelling down a waterfall in Puerto Vallarta, Mexico in 2015 for my 40th birthday.

Learning to surf in Waikiki, Hawaii, in 2012

White Water duckying on the Yough river in Pennsylvania in 2011

R2ing the Lower New River in West Virginia in 2011

FINDING MYSELF

Zip lining in Puerto Vallarta, Mexico

Hiking the Appalachian Trail in Virginia

Whitewater kayaking - Upper New River, WV

I started noticing that, at 38, the fairy tale was nowhere in sight. But it was also the first time I thought, maybe my fairy tale is just different. While I was having the time of my life and felt happy, I just wasn't meeting anyone that could provide me the relationship I thought I wanted. This is the first time I started thinking that maybe having a child on my own was going to be my reality. After meeting with a doctor to discuss my options I decided I would do it in the fall of that year. Well of course the fall came and went and I didn't go through with it. I guess there was still a hope that I'd meet "the one."

This is 40

I decided I'd wait until after my 40th birthday in 2015. I used the excuse this time that I could live up my 40th birthday year, do a triathlon (which I did), travel (I did that, too) and get that all out of my system and THEN have a child. Well, the fall came and went, and again, I didn't go through with it. But I also started panicking at this point. I was still living in the condo I bought when I was 28. It was not an ideal living situation for a baby due to the lack of rooms and plethora of steps, so my next excuse was, "I have to buy a house first." When in reality, I just wasn't ready and started to secretly wonder, did I really want a child, or was I just doing what society told me I was supposed to do? Because, all women are supposed to WANT to be moms, right?

But in the spring of 2016, when I was almost 41, I did follow through with my goal and sold my condo and bought a house. I was so proud of myself. I couldn't believe I bought a house all on my own, with no financial help from anyone. But honestly, it ended up as probably one of the most stressful times of my life. For a couple of reasons. Selling my condo with a $800 condo mortgage and moving to a house with double the square footage and double the price and expenses was one of them. I also had just discovered that the guy I had been dating during that time was a total sociopath and had lied about his entire existence (including the fact that he was engaged up until two weeks before meeting me online, his job, and the eight-ish or so other women he was sleeping with). I had weird gut feelings the entire time that something was "off" and this was the first time I actually acted on them by ending the relationship quickly as soon as my suspicions became true. I also had to move in with my mom for six weeks because my house closing didn't align with the sale of my condo. I was very grateful to my mom and her boyfriend Fred for letting me stay there. But once I got rid of that guy, got into the house and past the idea that a spirit was haunting it (a story for another time), I got comfortable and started being able to picture having a family. I had plenty of rooms, a beautiful yard and a great neighborhood. Most of all, I had faith in myself that I could do it. My self worth continued to grow.

    I thought Ok, I'm ready to move forward with baby. But the fall came, and again, I didn't go through with it. And again, I fell right back into old patterns and put it on hold again because I met someone. And within a few weeks, I realized that he had a substance abuse problem. I couldn't catch a break! Probably shouldn't have been surprised since we met drinking at a football tailgate. While we didn't date long, maybe six weeks or so, it was intense and important to mention since it again had me questioning my love for myself.

Jake was an alcoholic, and in denial. I brought it up to him after I witnessed him downing 12-15 glasses of whiskey in a night, continually cancelling plans and barely crawling out of bed at 10 or 11 a.m. on the weekends due to said partying, only to turn around and do it all again the next night. He ended up making me feel like I was the problem, because as he put it, I was "rigid and judgemental." And for awhile, which pisses me off now that I look back, I questioned whether or not that was true. Maybe he was right. Maybe it was me. Not him. I had become boring and settled. My expectations were too high that no one could live up to. He was just having fun and I was killing his buzz.

I gave him a second chance a couple months later because I believed he was right. But the second chance failed fast after he humiliated me after an evening together at his house. Convincing me that he missed me, he crawled on top of me and after approximately 1 minute (I'm not exaggerating), he finished, sat up and started flipping channels on the remote. I laid there, NAKED, in disbelief, feeling violated and disgusted and most of all, humiliated. I also lost it. I grabbed my clothes, got dressed, stormed out and cried as I drove home. The worst thing is, I blamed myself for the way everything went down. You see, I learned I do that because it's easier to blame myself because then I can fix it. If it's the guy's fault (in this case, his alcoholism), I can't fix that and it's therefore out of my control. Which I don't like.

What the fuck happened to my self worth I had spent all those years finding? While I had grown over the years to love myself more, there was — and probably always will be — a small ball of self-doubt that rears its ugly head sometimes when I least expect it. It's something I struggle with in my career and with goals I set, but it's something I especially struggle with when it comes to men. My heart still gets in the way of my head sometimes, too. I get caught up by chemistry. You see, my heart is my Achilles' heel. I so often, as you've read, see the "potential" in men — including this guy — in the beginning when they're on their best behavior. In my past, I fell fast and hard, and a man didn't even have to treat me well to get me to that point. My emotions and heart were theirs for the taking, and take they did. And I let them.

The good news is, after that episode, I never talked to him again. He reached out to me months later through text, and I ignored it. I had gotten my self worth back and wasn't about to lose it again.

Have you ever fallen back into old patterns, after you thought you had overcome them? If so, how?

How did you overcome it?

What do you do now to ensure you don't fall back into old patterns?

Do you struggle with self worth? If so, how?

How do you keep your self worth top of mind? If not top of mind, what can you do to make it a priority?

CHAPTER 6

Filling a void

In early 2017, at 41, I started feeling that the house was so overwhelming and my financial burden had doubled by becoming a homeowner, how would I possibly be able to afford to raise a child on my own? Then I started feeling bad about the house. Why did I buy an entire house? For just me? I mean, my cats love it but I sure as hell didn't buy a three bedroom house for me and two cats. The entire purpose of buying a house was so I could raise a child in it, in a nice neighborhood, with a yard. But meeting someone I could even stomach for more than a month wasn't happening, so I put the child idea away, again, thinking it just wasn't going to happen. I was really struggling with what I was supposed to do with my life at that point.

In September of 2017, I was feeling lost. I was thinking I wanted a relationship and I wanted to date. But I just wasn't meeting anyone that was worth a damn. But my friend Jennifer said something to me so profound one night at dinner, that it changed my life and my path forever.

"You've been searching for 'something' for so long, and I really don't think it's a guy. I think it's your child."

Right then and there, it had never been more clear. She was right. I had been searching. My entire life. For the wrong thing. It's always been about the child. I just never realized it more than in that moment. I had thought about it for years, but kept putting it off.

Had I been filling my life with all things fun to avoid facing the ultimate decision alone? Deciding to have a child by myself, in a way, was admitting defeat, that I couldn't find one guy who made me feel that he was capable of making me feel loved and secure enough that I'd be willing to have a child with him. But I was able to accept the fact that it just wasn't happening, and if I waited much longer, I was going to miss my opportunity of becoming a mother, which to me, was more important than becoming a wife.

But little did I know, I was about to experience the hardest time of my life.

FILLING A VOID

Have you ever had a profound epiphany moment? If so, what was it?

Did you act on it or not? Why?

CHAPTER 7

My Fertility Journey

When I returned from my Hawaiian vacation in October 2017, now age 42, I made an appointment to meet with a doctor at the local fertility clinic. I was excited but also nervous. After a brief conversation, he did a few blood tests to first make sure I was still capable of having a baby, and all was good. I had eggs and was ovulating regularly and my hormone levels were, I was told, like someone in their 30s.

I was told I would go through what is called Intrauterine Insemination (IUI). Basically the turkey baster method, but by putting a really small tube filled with sperm all the way up into your uterus to give you the best chance. This means the spermies are closer to the eggies and don't have to make the extra journey through your vagina and cervix. Great! Sounds like a piece of cake!

When the doctor called to tell me to start my fertility meds on day three of my cycle, I was like, "Um, excuse me? Fertility meds? Why do I need those if

I'm ovulating on my own?" Turns out doctors want to "boost" your chances and apparently these drugs are supposed to do that. So I just went ahead with it, which is very unlike me not to question something like that. But when you're dependent on a doctor and a specialist's advice, especially for solo motherhood, you kind of give them all your trust and just go with it. (Now that I've been through what I've been through and I look back at that time, this is something I wish I would've pushed back on in the beginning. More on that later.) So I started a fertility pill on day three of my cycle and after three days of taking it, ugh, I felt like fucking hell. Dizzy, brain fog, couldn't form any thoughts and was so fatigued. I only had to take it for five days total, but it felt like a lifetime.

Then came time to order donor sperm. I got sticker shock immediately when I saw the one vial — which equaled one try — was $700. Yep, $700 folks! I immediately started wondering who I knew that might consider $200 for a donation. But then I realized that person would be in my life, and my child's forever, so I quickly got over the $700 shock.

Ordering donor sperm online is pretty much like online dating. You see the donor's photos (but only if you buy them, because after all, you want to be sure they don't look like a monster), you read an essay he wrote on why you should pick him, and you get to see how tall he is, the color of his hair and eyes, and learn about his favorite hobbies. One perk is you do get access to his medical history, which shows you when his grandparents died and from what horrible disease. Sometimes I think it might be better to go in blind. After all, isn't that what most people do anyway? But then again, maybe I should've been asking all the previously mentioned guys in this book for their essays.

The donor process is pretty crazy to me. The good news, which I never knew before, is that a man can't just walk in and donate sperm one time just because he feels like earning $50 one day. It's a pretty serious, involved process where these sperm banks recruit young college kids and "enroll" them in the program for a certain amount of time, or until they've hit their max allowed number of pregnancies. It's pretty crazy. I often wonder if these guys grow up and at age 40 end up having major regrets about what they did to earn money during college. But I've also heard that men love to spread their seed, so there's that.

So I scrolled and scrolled through endless profiles until I settled on one super adorable guy who looked like he was 18 who had a great medical history. But I felt oddly gross and like a creepy old lady. My mom even said, "Can't you find someone *a little* older?" I quickly reminded my mom that I wasn't dating him, that I was just using his sperm and the younger and faster the sperm the better!

A few days before I was supposed to ovulate, the doctor had me come in for an ultrasound to see how I had responded to the meds. I had one great mature egg as planned, and I was then told to give myself the "trigger shot" that evening, and then we'd do the IUI 36 hours later.

Let me tell you. The first time I did that trigger shot was awful. The trigger shot is actually HCG hormone (otherwise known as pregnancy hormone that women's bodies create once they're actually pregnant). The goal is to inject yourself in the stomach with it at 9 p.m. at night, which then forces you to ovulate around 36 hours later, which is when they inseminate you during the IUI. It's all about the perfect timing, you see.

The problem with the shot is you have to mix it up yourself and get it into the needle ... something that doctors usually do FOR you. Nope. Not this time. I had to do it myself. Well, I thought I was prepared and I had the worst time getting the liquid out of the vial and back into the shot! I was freaking out and had called a friend to help me. I finally figured out that I was putting the needle too far into the vial and wasn't pulling any of the liquid out. I swear I lost a ton of the fluid all over the sink and am pretty sure I injected myself with a tube full of air.

The morning of the IUI, I, along with my super amazing, supportive mom and her boyfriend, went to the sperm bank at 7:30 a.m. to sign a release form. The bank then unthawed the sperm and "washed" it, meaning, they use a special fluid to separate the slow sperm from the fast ones and remove the seminal fluid altogether. I had 1.5 hours to kill so we just went to have breakfast, then headed to the clinic at 9 a.m. for the IUI. Apparently that Saturday morning everyone in the city was trying to make a baby the same way I was because the waiting room was packed! And somehow I managed to be the last one called at almost 10 a.m.! The IUI took all of 2 minutes, but on my drive home, I got very crampy and almost passed out from my nerves. I had to hop in the back seat and let my mom's boyfriend drive me home. I was a hot mess. I went home and slept most of the rest of the day.

The next two weeks were stressful. Waiting to find out if I was pregnant and judging every little twinge and symptom, and then googling said symptoms, it was making me crazy! And I had a ton of symptoms. Crampy. Nauseated. Tired. I swore it worked.

Nope. Negative. Didn't work.

I actually wasn't upset the first time the IUI failed. Everything I had read prepared me for the fact that the first IUI wouldn't work. So I set up to try again the very next month. Maybe just maybe, it will be a

Christmas surprise. I decided to use the same donor and started the fertility meds and hell feeling again two weeks later. I did my second IUI via the same process on Dec. 8, 2017.

And holy shit, it worked!

During that two week wait, I had no symptoms at all and felt normal. I was SURE it failed. I remember sitting at my grandma's house a few days before I tested, and I remember getting a weird hot flash for a brief period of time and had a few sharp twinges near my uterine area. (Looking back, I now know that those symptoms were actually implantation, where the embryo was implanting itself into the wall of my uterus.)

Two days before I was "supposed" to test, I had been texting with my friend Emily who had just had a baby and was still in the hospital. She said "Test now so you can find out on the day I had my baby!" I remember telling her that I was sure I wasn't pregnant because I had zero symptoms. I went ahead anyway and two lines immediately came up. I was like HOLY SHIT, IT'S POSITIVE!" I was laughing and trembling and called some of my closest friends and my mom, as they all were super supportive during the entire process.

I couldn't believe it — it worked on the second try! The doctor had me go right away to get a blood test to test the level of HCG pregnancy hormone in my blood, which should be at a level of 50 or more at that time. Mine came back at 57, which seemed low, but they said as long as it was at least 50, I was good. Then I was told I needed to go back every two days to make sure it doubled, as HCG is supposed to double every 48-72 hours to show a healthy pregnancy. Since Christmas was that weekend, my family and I were ecstatic at the Christmas news and it was an exciting and unbelievable time.

Two days later I went back for the blood test, only to find out the HCG level had only hit 90, when it should have been over 100, then two days later when it should have been 200, it was only 157.

The nurse told me that I'd have to go test again in two days, but that if it didn't double, it was probably a chemical pregnancy and I'd just start my period, so basically, an early miscarriage. I was in shock and became super depressed. What just happened??

So two days later I went back, and the level had jumped to 350, then 700, then to over 1,000! It looked like I was in the clear and the embryo had finally latched on. However, I was a ball of nerves during that entire time and felt like something was off.

The Miscarriage

My miscarriage happened the weekend of Jan. 12, 2018, Martin Luther King, Jr. holiday weekend, even though I know now I had started miscarrying in the days leading up to it. Most likely the baby actually passed away a week prior. I clearly remember having a weird pinching and was also having some brown spotting about a week prior, so I went to the doctor to get an early ultrasound to mainly make sure it wasn't ectopic (stuck in my fallopian tube). He did the ultrasound and we could see the confirmed pregnancy. I was ecstatic! He said the spotting was normal but we just had to see how things go.

Well, sure enough, the next day, the spotting turned red. I decided to work at home the next day so I could stay off my feet and rest. That morning, I remember having terrible back pain and laying on a heating pad. I got up to go to the bathroom and discovered a LOT of blood. My heart dropped. I knew exactly what was happening.

I think I must have been in a weird calm shock, because I ended up driving to Kroger to get Maxi pads. There was also a snow storm coming so everyone and their mother was there getting milk and bread for the coming snow apocalypse and I was standing in line trying to look and remain calm with cramps, toilet paper and maxi pads, all while in the middle of my miscarriage.

Once I made it home I started having contraction-type cramps for a few hours. I called the doctor on call and since I didn't have a fever and wasn't "hemorrhaging," he had me come in the next day for an ultrasound. He confirmed that I had in fact lost the baby. I broke down in the nurse's office, pulled myself together and drove home. I got home, took a hot shower, got on a heating pad and took a lot of Aleve. And cried with my mom and her boyfriend by my side. That night, I had a dream that a little girl with Down syndrome walked up to me with a balloon and smiled, and then walked away. I fully believe that was my daughter I had just lost. It was such a cold, sad weekend filled with emotional and physical pain. I remember it like it was yesterday.

As I sat there on my couch, physically and emotionally suffering through a miscarriage at eight weeks along, I didn't know what to do with myself. I tried to sleep, watch TV, to cuddle with my fur babies, but nothing took away the fact that I just lost the most precious thing I had wanted more than anything in my life. Something I had been planning on and off for years. So I wrote. I wrote a blog and shared it on my social sites, because I felt like someone had to break the stigma and I wasn't going to just have a miscarriage and not try to help someone else, or myself, through it. I was amazed at how many people, both men and women, commented with their experience with miscarriage. It was incredibly honest and brave of everyone.

I'm now part of a club I never thought I'd be a part of. The 1 in 4 women who lose their babies before they get to hold them in their arms. I kept telling myself miscarriage is common and a body's way of getting rid of something unhealthy (and I've heard that from others, too, and I've said that to other women before I went through this), but I realize now those are things that should never be said to a woman going through this. The best thing to say to someone going through this is "I'm sorry, I'm here for you." No matter how much "our bodies do what's right" it doesn't take away the gut-wrenching pain and mental anguish of hopes and dreams vanishing in the blink of an eye. They say from the time a woman sees two pink lines she bonds with that child. I can say that is true.

MIscarriages are hard to talk about. There's a weird failure feeling that comes with it that you can't really explain. It feels like you failed, your body failed. Even though you did everything perfectly you start thinking, "Did I walk too fast this morning, did I strain too much going to the bathroom, did I take too hot of a bath, did I eat something too spicy." The list goes on and on and on, and reality is, SHIT HAPPENS! Most likely the pregnancy wasn't healthy and your body actually did the RIGHT thing. It's so important though for all women to talk about if they can so other women know they're not alone, to know that miscarriage is actually unbelievably common, unfortunately.

I can honestly say this was the one thing in my life that made me understand that I needed to lean on my friends and family. And God am I grateful for the amazing people in my life: the ones who called, emailed, texted, hugged me, cooked me breakfast and fed me, my mom and sister who sat with me and stayed on the phone with me and sobbed while I sobbed. I may have been strong but my heart was broken and it forever changed me.

PADDLING UPSTREAM

Have you or your partner ever had a miscarriage? If so, how far along were you?

_____
_____
_____
_____

Did you talk openly about it or keep it to yourself? Why or why not?

_____
_____
_____
_____

Did you have a support system? If so, how did they help you through it?

_____
_____
_____
_____

CHAPTER 8

Picking myself up

After the miscarriage and my hormone levels fell, so did my mental state. I was depressed. I was tired and sad. So sad. It took me months to feel hopeful again. My body naturally miscarried, meaning, I didn't need medical assistance. For that I am grateful. My body bounced back quickly and ovulated on time and on schedule the very next month. The doctor wanted me to take that month off from trying, but said I could try in March. Mentally I can now say I wasn't ready. But back then, all I could think about was trying again because everything you read says how "fertile" you are after a miscarriage. So I tried again in March and April and nothing happened. Except I got depressed again. I decided at that point to take a three-month break for emotional and financial purposes. I decided that bike riding, kayaking and drinking on patios during the summer was a little more appealing to get my mind right. I also needed a break from putting my body through the wringer of fertility pills, a miscarriage, ultrasounds and other invasive procedures.

In July, I had some additional invasive, painful tests done, like having a tube of dye shot through my uterus and fallopian tubes — which was just an absolute blast — that showed everything was normal and healthy, so I was excited and hopeful. No known issues. So I tried again in August in September. And both times, yea, you guessed it, BIG FAT NEGATIVES.

When the sixth IUI failed in September 2018, I just completely lost my shit. I got mad at my body for failing me. I got mad at the clinic for continually making me do IUIs when I felt we should have moved to IVF (In Vitro Fertilization). I felt like a failure and was so frustrated all I could do was scream. I decided to make an appointment with my doctor to discuss next steps and to talk about IVF. But I also decided I finally needed to get a second opinion from a different clinic. So I made an appointment for Nov. 5 with a new doctor at the Cleveland Clinic in Cleveland, Ohio, one of the best medical facilities in the country.

October 2018

I met with my doctor one last time in Columbus to get some guidance from him. While he was a really nice doctor, he was not very aggressive or helpful in helping me decide next steps. I asked him directly why we were doing so many IUIs at this point, because my age was against me, and why have we not yet talked about IVF?

Side note: Frozen donor sperm, once thawed, only lives for 12 hours. Fresh sperm, like when a couple has sex, can live for three to five DAYS. This means that when doing IUI, I had a 12-hour window to get pregnant, and if I ovulated outside of that window, what do you think happens? Nothing. That's what. The problem is that while I WAS ovulating, there was no exact way to know if I was ovulating within that 12-hour window. It's just their best "guess" medically. This is why I was getting frustrated with my doctor. At 43, I don't have time to waste with these IUIs that are literally a shot in the dark.

He pushed me to do a 7th IUI. Told me that I was healthy and I got pregnant once, that it's just a "matter of time" until we find that one good egg. And he really didn't think I "needed" to go through the invasive procedure of IVF because it was very expensive. However, the amount of money I had spent on IUIs was quickly approaching the cost of one round of IVF.

I was so frustrated because the extra meds with a 7th IUI cycle were $500 out of pocket. Oh, and donor sperm? $700 each try. The IUI, blood work and ultrasounds? Between $700 and $1,000. One more IUI equaled about $2,000 give or take.

To encourage me to try one more IUI rather than IVF, he said he'd give me the $500 meds for free. Wow, for free?! I immediately perked up! That's amazing! So they gave me the meds and I went back to work. I threw the meds into my lunch bag, because there was a cold pack in there, and they had to be kept cold since they had been refrigerated at my doctor's office so they'd have a longer shelf life.

That evening, I got home and threw my lunch bag in the freezer to refreeze the cold pack. But guess what else I froze? And ruined? And didn't realize it until the next morning when I woke up in a cold-sweat panic? The meds. That's right. I just ruined $500 of free fertility meds. I know all of you that have had to use those meds are cringing right now because you know how fucking expensive a tiny vial of that medicine is.

I immediately started googling, "Frozen follistim" and everything that came up said, "Ruined," or "No longer good." I called the doctor and the pharmacy and they delivered the same news Google had unveiled to me earlier.

I was so defeated and depressed that evening, I just couldn't believe it. But it was just the first sign I needed to realize I didn't need to do the 7th IUI.

PICKING MYSELF UP

As I was getting ready to leave on a weekend getaway with the girls the next day, I got a surprise $1,200 medical bill in the mail for one of the tests I had in July. A test that I called the insurance company about in June to confirm it was covered. They confirmed that it would be covered since it was a diagnostic test. I immediately called them and the doctor and was basically like, "WHAT THE FUCK!" I pitched a huge fit and promptly walked into my garage to let out the biggest "I'm losing it" scream of my life. LIterally. I screamed. Full force. I thought my head was going to pop off. My anxiety was so high at that point I didn't know what to do with myself. It was right then and there I decided I could not in my right mind do a 7th IUI and incur $2,000 more in medical expenses for a 5% chance that it would work this time.

The ruined meds and the medical bill, in my mind, was the universe's way of telling me to "STOP." So I did.

Has anything set you off so much that you completely lost it? If so, what was it?

_____
_____
_____
_____

Have you ever had clear signs to take a different path? If so, what were they?

_____
_____
_____
_____

Did you listen? Why or why not?

_____
_____
_____
_____

CHAPTER 9

IVF

When I first started trying to have a baby on my own, I said, "I'll do three IUIs and if it doesn't work, I'll stop." I was naive as hell. Six IUIs and a miscarriage had woken up the motherly instinct inside of me and now I didn't feel like quitting was an option. So I decided I would do IVF — In Vitro Fertilization. And instead of doing it here where I lived, I decided I would go to the Cleveland Clinic in Beachwood two hours away, since I was informed they had a better lab than the fertility clinic I had gone to for the IUIs. I figured if I'm going to do IVF and go through all of that, I wasn't going to go somewhere that had a half-ass lab. I was going to go to the best and I was sure it was going to work.

In the middle of all of this, just to make things even more chaotic, I decided to change jobs for a new opportunity. Unbelievably, a week after I accepted the role in November 2018, I found out the new company had insurance coverage for fertility treatments.

I remember finding that out right before bed one night and tears streaming down my cheeks. What an absolute godsend, since it costs about $15,000 for one round of IVF. I felt lucky and extremely grateful, as most companies don't offer fertility coverage and most couples and women were paying expenses out of pocket. And I had already spent more than $10,000 out of pocket in 2018 just doing the IUIs, since I had no insurance fertility benefits at that time. I thought, "This HAS to be sign. I was meant to get this job so I could do IVF to have my baby!" Everything was finally aligning.

Round I of IVF was exciting. I was sure it was going to work, especially since I ended up at a job that had insurance coverage for it. I had plenty of eggs left, my hormone levels still looked good, and there was no reason it wouldn't now, since the lab was involved in fertilizing my eggs and getting them to the proper stage where they could be transferred back to me. Easy right?

The doctor told me we'd probably be able to retrieve six eggs, because of my age, and I told her I bet we'd get 10-12. But before I tell you the result, I feel like I would be doing every woman who's gone through IVF a disservice if I didn't share the full details of what a round of IVF — complete with egg retrieval and transfer — is like.

IVF Prep

My IVF prep was pretty standard and I was lucky enough to be what they call a "good responder" since my hormone levels were still pretty good, in fact, like someone in their 30s. For the first two weeks I took birth control pills. Sounds counterintuitive right? The pills allows the doctor to control your cycle, ensures your ovaries start producing follicles evenly (follicles are what contain each egg) and it also helps prevent cysts later on when you're injecting yourself with insane amounts of hormones to grow an insane amount of eggs.

After the pills ended, I started twice-a-day stomach injections of a medicine called Lupron, which does two things: wakes your ovaries up as they get ready for the hormone injections, but it also helps to ensure that while you're injecting said hormones, you don't accidentally ovulate early before the retrieval.

After one to two days of Lupron, I started stomach injections of FSH (Follicle Stimulating Hormone), which is what we women naturally produce in order to ovulate. However, I was injecting a lot of it, twice a day, to produce numerous eggs, instead of the one we naturally produce every month.

During the eight days of injections, I had to go to the lab every other day at 7 a.m. for bloodwork to ensure my estrogen level was at the right level, not too high, not too low, and then I drove to a local fertility clinic immediately afterward for my 8 a.m. vaginal ultrasound to see how the follicles were growing. Once at least two of the follicles reach 18mm, they tell you to inject the trigger shot at a specific time on a specific night, to get ready for the retrieval 36 hours later.

Sounds fun, right? Let me tell you how "fun" IVF is:

Retrieval

Retrieval day was exciting and scary. My mom had spent the night with me since we had to head to Cleveland Clinic at 5 a.m., to be there by 7 a.m. My retrieval would be at 8 a.m. Once we arrived, I got checked in, hooked up to an IV, signed a waiver since I was being put to sleep, to ensure I wouldn't sue anyone if I died, and then was wheeled into the operating room.

Now that was some crazy shit. The embryologist and IVF lab was literally connected to the operating room, via a doorway that looks like an order window at a restaurant. There were numerous test tubes lined up on a table, just waiting to accept the eggs that the doctor removed from me.

As they lay me back on the operating bed, they pull my legs up and strap them in so I'm literally flat on my back with my legs at a 90 degree angle, in all my glory. At that moment, all I could think about was that I was happy I had shaved. I remember feeling so cold that my legs were trembling, to which the nurse informed me that was probably just nerves. They quickly started making small talk with me to get my mind off of what was happening, and the next thing I knew, I woke up about 25 minutes later. The deed had been done.

So what is the deed you ask? How exactly are those eggies retrieved? Well, the doctor basically puts a needle through your vagina wall and into your ovaries, pulling out the fluid (which contains an egg most of the time) from each follicle. Then it goes into the test tubes lined up on the table. Sounds barbaric right? That's because it is. Luckily I was knocked out with Fentanyl for it and don't remember a thing.

Recovery

IVF recovery is an interesting thing. Basically your ovaries are swollen and full of fluid and trying to heal from being poked and prodded. So not only do you feel exhausted from spending the last two weeks injecting hormones into your body, your own body is releasing 10 times the amount of hormones after ovulation (in my case, after the egg retrieval). So you're mentally loopy, physically a wreck and look five months pregnant from the bloat.

Post-retrieval lab phone calls

This is honestly the worst part, mentally, of IVF. Once your eggs are retrieved, the lab immediately tries to fertilize them and then everyone waits until the next morning to see which ones made a love connection. The lab calls you that morning to tell you how many eggs fertilized, which can be anywhere from all of them to none of them. It's reported that an average of 70% of retrieved eggs fertilize. So for example, if you get 10 eggs retrieved, you can expect about seven of them to survive the first night. Then the lab proceeds to call you every morning for the next four mornings to tell you which fertilized embryos divided properly to the needed number of cells to be considered "viable." It is honestly the most nerve-wracking feeling to wait for a phone call to see if any of your embryos survived the hunger games each day.

Transfer

If you're lucky enough to have any embryos survive the hunger games and make it to day five, you then move to the next phase — the coveted transfer of the embryo back to the uterus. This is a very exciting time, as you've just made it through both physical and mental torture.

There are two types of transfers in IVF:

Fresh – When an embryo is transferred back to a woman's uterus three to give days after the egg retrieval.

Frozen – When an embryo is frozen after developing in the lab for five days after the egg retrieval, frozen and stored for transfer back to the woman's uterus at a later date.

Two Week Wait

After the embryo is transferred to the woman's uterus, you then have to wait a grueling two weeks to take a pregnancy test to see if that little sucker implanted. You see, a lot of people don't realize it but IVF follows the same timeline as if an egg was fertilized in a woman's body naturally. The first five days in the lab are like the first five days in the fallopian tube. The fertilized egg has to divide into a certain number of cells every day for five days until it makes it down into the uterus, where it will then attempt to implant into the wall of the uterus so it can develop over the next nine months until it's born. So when an embryo is transferred back into the uterus in IVF, it seems like it should just implant with no problem and work, RIGHT?! Wrong! It fails all the time and honestly doctors have no idea really, why some embryos implant and why some don't, and that's both naturally and via IVF.

Test

So after symptom spotting and reading 999,9999 TTC (trying to conceive) discussion boards online daily for two weeks on the interwebs, seeing if any other women experienced nipple twinges and lightening crotch, you have to get a pregnancy blood test at the lab. OR, you can do what most women do, take a home test way too early and break down sobbing for days, only to have to still get the lab blood test for final confirmation, adding insult to injury.

So back to my retrieval ...

IVF

My Result

We got 10 eggs, ha! I knew it! Six eggs my ass. The doctor was totally wrong about me. I may have been 43, but I was a fit energetic 43 who was often mistaken for being in her 30s. That had to mean my ovaries didn't look or act their age either, right? I imagined them looking all young, with no wrinkles, just pushing out the eggs like champs. Yea. Well. I quickly realized that while my ovaries may look like life hadn't worn them down, my eggs had become a little hard boiled.

You see, as I said above, after the eggs are retrieved, the lab attempts to fertilize them. And, not all of the eggs are always "mature," and if they're not, they're pretty much toast immediately. I ended up with seven mature eggs out of the 10; out of the seven, only four fertilized. Four?! Four.

I went from 10 to four in one day. ONE DAY! Then for the next five days, the lab called me each morning to tell me which of the embryos lived to see another day — remember, the embryo hunger games? The embryo's cells have to divide properly once the egg is fertilized, just as they would in inside the body, until day five or six, where it then is capable of implanting inside your uterus.

Well out of the four, one made it to day five. One. ONE! Out of 10. Apparently this is normal. And the fact that I had 10 retrieved and one make it to day five, well, apparently for my age, well, that was a triumph.

I was so devastated but also grateful to get one, as I didn't want to get to the end of this and have nothing to transfer back to me to see if it would stick around. Since I had to do what is known as a frozen transfer because my hormone levels had gotten too high (dangerous to do a fresh transfer as you can get very sick), I had a month to recover from the hormones. Only I didn't really have that time, because a few weeks later I was sticking giant PIO (progesterone in oil) shots in my ass and taking estrogen pills to make sure my uterine lining was perfect for the embryo transfer— again, mimicking the stages if you had gotten pregnant naturally.

IVF

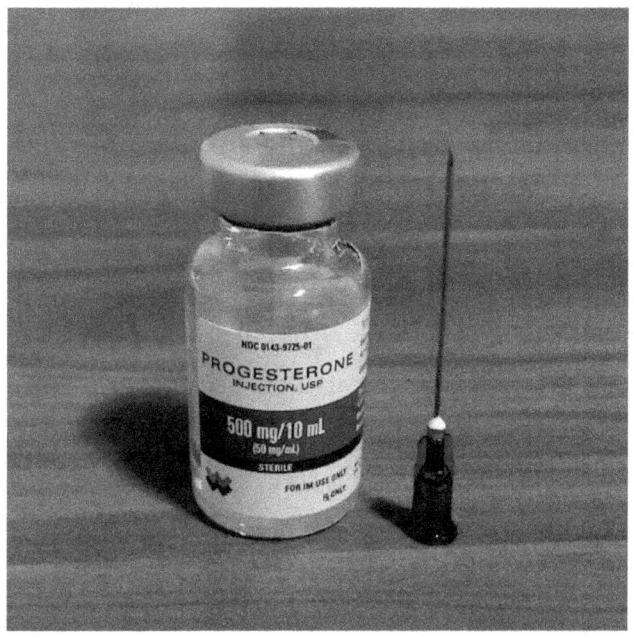

Progesterone in oil and the needle I had to
use to inject it into my ass cheek.

So a month later, I drove up to Cleveland *again* to welcome my one lone embryo home to where it belonged — my uterus. The transfer went flawlessly and took about five minutes. I drove home from Cleveland yet again and waited for two weeks to take the test, only to find out it had failed.

My first IVF cycle had failed.

I was defeated. Bloated. Tired. Hormonal. 10 lbs. heavier. And pissed. I cried, screamed and had some panic attacks. No one gave me a reason why other than "probably my age" as the doctor said. But it fails all the time, even for younger women, and all they say is, "We don't know why." I didn't blame anyone, but I was mad that I had all these eggs in my body, when many women at this age don't anymore, but none of them seemed to be viable. I seem to be able to make embryos, but they don't seem to want to stick around. Is it my uterus? Does my body reject them as a foreign invader? Are they chromosomally abnormal? No one knows. It's all a crapshoot.

The same day the doctor called to tell me my blood test was negative and I wasn't pregnant, she immediately tried to convince me to use a donor egg. Talk about lack of empathy. "I'm sorry it didn't work, but if you spend $30,000 you can use a younger woman's eggs and we can fertilize them with $700 of sperm and then see if one of those embryos implants in your uterus." For God's sake, can you give me a couple days to grieve before trying to push someone else's eggs down my throat (and into my uterus)?

IVF

Has a doctor ever disregarded your feelings? If so, about what?

If you have gone through IVF, what was your experience with the first round? Was it successful or not?

If not, did you try again? Why or why not?

CHAPTER 10

Round Two

> I AM SEEKING, I AM STRIVING,
> I AM IN IT WITH ALL MY HEART.
>
> VINCENT VAN GOGH

A framed message my friends Becky and Chad gave me right before my second round of IVF in June 2019.

I reluctantly decided to go for round two with my own eggs in June 2019. Mentally I was worn down, and was really tired of subjecting my body to mass amounts of meds that messed me up mentally and physically. But I still had an insurance benefit left so I felt like I just couldn't walk away after one round of IVF. After all, I just had to buy that pesky sperm again for $700 and then $1,200 worth of meds. To put it in perspective, if I didn't have insurance, it would've cost me about $15,000 for a cycle. So I got off cheap.

Round two was a little better on me in all ways. My doctor and I decided that since I had plenty of eggs, we'd use less medicine and try to get better *quality* eggs, instead of going for a max amount of eggs with a max dose. I'd probably get less eggs retrieved than last time, but maybe, just maybe, I'd get some that were better quality and not scrambled. So all through the eight days of injections, I felt so much better and didn't gain as much weight. But I think in a lot of ways it was better because I knew in my heart and mind that it was the final cycle, whether it succeeded or failed, because I just couldn't put myself through it anymore. I wanted my life back.

My mom and I drove two hours up to the clinic again on the day of the retrieval. Luckily this time I didn't need to be there until 11 a.m. The doctor still ended up retrieving 11 eggs, so I was ecstatic since it was one more than the first time! But the next day, the embryologist called to tell me that only five were mature, which means only five were viable. What?! Five? Out of 11? I freaked at first because there were so few mature eggs, but my doctor reminded me that was the goal, less eggs that were viable but better quality. Ok, yea, she was right. That was the goal, but secretly I was hoping I just had an amazing cycle and my body was finally showing everyone how healthy and capable it was.

After I accepted that news, I just remember being so glad the retrieval part of the cycle was done and I was having a better recovery since we used less meds. I was overall less stressed going into the five-day embryo hunger games again. That is until I got the call that informed me that only three of the five embryos made it to day three, and I still had two more days to go!

So as I'm freaking out those two days, I then had to start more meds for the fresh transfer that was taking place on day five of any embryos that survived. I had to get my uterus ready to accept an embryo, basically making sure it had the right environment to implant itself. So not only was I coming off hormones injections, I was putting them back in by taking oral estrogen pills and vagionally inserting progesterone pellets. Keeps getting better doesn't it? I mean, it was just a total blast all around.

Day five rolled around and I drove two hours up to the clinic *again* for the transfer of the one embryo that made it. I was once again thrilled just to have one chance. But to my surprise, once I got into the doctor's office, the doctor told me I had TWO to transfer! I was in total shock and excited that now I had two chances. It just had to work this time!

As I drove home with my embryos snuggling up in my uterus, I imagined (and slightly freaked out about) having twins. Maybe they'd be a boy and a girl, Willow and Jude, or maybe I'd have two girls who would drive me crazy as teenagers. But I'd also be OK with one — one healthy baby. I was honestly just excited to be hopeful again.

As the two-week wait commenced, I decided to live my life as normal as possible and not get overly excited. I was tired of being hard on myself and trying to do everything perfectly, as all the perfect stuff I had done the past 1.5 years didn't work. At the end of the two weeks, like last time, I had to get a blood test and wait for the result from the doctor. However, this time, I decided I couldn't put myself through waiting on a call again, so I took a home test the day before the blood test. NEGATIVE.

Honestly, I knew in my heart it was going to be negative, before it was negative. I have never told anyone this, but during those two weeks, I had moments where I felt like I just wasn't meant to birth a child. At least not like this. It was almost like a premonition. Maybe that's why I took the home test before the blood test this time. I just knew, and I wanted to prepare myself before the doctor called. I also knew, that after 1.5 years and eight attempts, I was finally done.

Have you ever had a premonition that something wasn't going to "your way"? If so, what about?

Have you done fertility treatments and decided to stop?

Do you regret your decision? Why or why not?

CHAPTER 11

Why I chose to stop fertility treatments

1.5: Years spent trying to have a baby on my own through fertility treatments

6: Number of IUIs I did from Nov. 2017 - Aug. 2018.

1: Number of pregnancies and miscarriages (Jan. 2018) I had from above IUIs

2: Rounds of IVF and embryo transfers, that failed in April and June 2019

150+: Number of fertility pills I took and shots I injected into my stomach and hip for IVF

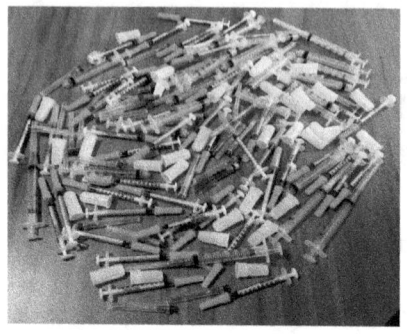

Photo of two rounds of IVF shots

1,000+ (lost track): Number of supplements and pills I took to improve egg quality

75+: Number of acupuncture treatments I had for fertility

100+: Number of doctor appointments I had during 1.5 years of treatments

0: The number of babies that resulted from 1.5 years of hellish fertility treatments.

After 1.5 years of trying to become a single mother by choice, by artificial measures, and going to so many doctors appts and blood draws that accompany IUIs and IVF cycles that I lost track, I decided to stop. Not only did it take a physical toll on my body and a financial toll on my wallet, the emotional toll was the worst. I just couldn't put myself through it anymore. Honestly, I felt a huge sense of relief to stop the madness, to take the weight and pressure off myself, and to just accept what is.

As you get older, it gets harder to get pregnant, as only about 10-20% of our eggs are still considered viable. I thought I'd defeat the odds. I can't tell you how many times I heard, "You're so healthy you'll get pregnant fast," (I did get pregnant on the second try but had a miscarriage at 8 weeks) or, "If you can't get pregnant as fit as you are I'm not sure who can." I thought so, too, honestly. But the reality is, it has nothing to do with that. It has everything to do with age, and at this age (44 as of June 2019) IVF is only about 3-5% effective (and only 30-40% for younger women). Getting pregnant naturally is actually more likely at my age, but in order for that to happen, you have to have a partner, and I do not right now, by choice. Bringing a child into this world with a half-ass partner just hasn't been appealing. I find it so ironic now that I spent most of my life trying to prevent pregnancy.

When I got the test result that the two-embryos transferred to me as part of my second IVF cycle failed to implant, honestly it wasn't a surprise. I just didn't believe at that point it was going to work after the uphill battle I had experienced during the entire journey. It's like I knew in my gut it was time to be done. I was so exhausted mentally and physically that I just wanted to be done and move on with my life, as I felt that I had put it on hold for 1.5 years. The emotional roller coaster and stress of fertility treatments is actually said to be comparable to having cancer or heart disease. I've never had either one of those, but I can attest to the fact that it is brutal, depressing, heart wrenching and absolutely gutting, and what I've been through is something that can't be understood if you haven't been through it. It really has the ability to steal your joy and fill it instead with stress, anxiety and depression. It's extremely isolating.

And that's why I decided to stop. I needed my happiness back. I needed to find joy in my daily life again without counting out the number of supplements I had to take, when the next blood draw or doctor appointment was, being up in the morning and home at a certain time at night to make sure I was doing the five shots/day in my stomach at just the right time, putting new estrogen patches on my stomach every other day, dealing with brain fog and hormonal weight gain, sticking progesterone supplements up my "vajayjay" and a 1.5 inch needle into my ass every morning to make sure my progesterone was super high to support a pregnancy, giving myself bruises and knots that were so painful I could barely sit down. All of that while working and trying to keep my shit together.

WHY I CHOSE TO STOP FERTILITY TREATMENTS

NO MORE. I chose to stop. I chose to take my power back.

That day I chose myself. I chose my mental and physical wellness. I chose to be grateful for what I do have in my life. An amazing family who has been in this 100% with me, including my mom who went to almost every doctor appointment with me — even the ones two hours away — friends who have supported me for 1.5 years by sharing in my excitement and the heart-wrechning failure each and every time, and nieces and nephews who I love very much and have made me a happy aunt (I'm a pretty good one by the way), a great career and a comfortable home. and of course my kit cats!

I am so proud of myself, for my resilience and strength, for never missing a day of work while going through treatments no matter how shitty I felt, for crying into my pillow (and wine) and getting up the next day and putting on a brave face for work and the world, and for being open and sharing my story in hopes that this struggle isn't hidden anymore and that women start sharing their experiences so other women know they're not alone.

If you know anyone who is struggling with infertility, just give them a hug and ask how they're doing. That means everything. But here's what not to do:

1. Don't tell them "Kids are expensive anyway, you don't want them."
2. At least you don't have to go through labor or birth and you'll have your body intact."
3. You can borrow my kids anytime!
4. At least you can travel now.
5. You can always adopt — for $30,000.

Just don't say anything like this. Please?

I will never know what it feels like to be pregnant (with the exception of the eight weeks I had before the miscarriage), to buy cute maternity clothes, to feel a baby kick, to give birth and see my baby for the first time laying on my chest. I will never have a biological child. Those are the painful thoughts that go through my head, that make me cry as I sit here typing them.

But I know I am and will always be OK. I process things by opening up about them and I knew that healing meant talking about and sitting with my grief. Once I get back to 100% (I'm almost there) and back to enjoying life fully again without fertility treatments ruling my schedule, I may look into adoption or fostering a child who needs someone who can show them love and happiness, even if it's just for a short time. Or, maybe I'll just keep focusing on being an awesome aunt for my nieces and nephews, and for my friends' children. Maybe that's always been my path. I heard someone say once that some women are meant to be moms, some women are meant to be aunts and some neither. I think being an aunt might just be what I'm meant to be.

Which category do you fall into? Mom, aunt or neither?

Do you wish you were one or the other? Why or why not?

CHAPTER 12

The climb to get my life back

As soon as I decided to stop treatments, there was a surge of excitement and a feeling of 1,000 pounds being lifted off my shoulders. I was ready to reclaim my life and get back to doing the things I loved: biking, hiking, kayaking, traveling, drinking wine without worrying about the possibility of being pregnant, and setting goals for myself again other than trying to produce more and more eggs and embryos every month. I took the remaining summer months of 2019 and lived my life to the fullest. Theme parks, water parks, lake trips, bike rides, drinks with friends, hanging with family — I pretty much just shoved as much as I could into the last two months of summer, since I had lost so much of my life and freedom over the previous 1.5 years. There's still not one ounce of me that regrets stopping treatment.

But while I was ready to reclaim my life after the second IVF fail, my body had a different idea. You see, while I was trying to get pregnant, the fertility clinic put me on a thyroid medicine to lower my TSH (thyroid stimulating hormone) to give me a better shot at getting pregnant. While my thyroid was at normal levels already, they wanted it even lower. So I went on the first prescription I had ever been on, on a consistent basis. But when I decided to stop with treatments after round two had failed, I also decided to stop taking all meds and supplements cold turkey, as I didn't need them anymore, and I wasn't being monitored anymore by a doctor since I had stopped treatments.

Well, that was a big mistake. The weird physical ailments I had to deal with post-treatment included numbness in my face and shoulder, leg fatigue in both legs, overall fatigue and just being unenergized, weird electrical shocks in my forearms on and off, 2-3 inch weight gain in my stomach just to name a few. Considering I'm a pretty serious fitness and wellness guru, gaining weight and feeling like crap for months has been very scary. My doctors said I most likely had a hormone imbalance and that I just have to "wait it out" and let my body work it out and eventually I'll get back to normal. Easy for them to say.

I was barely able to bike 5 miles when I was used to biking 25. I was also so tired all the time I could barely get up in the morning and get myself together to go to work. I also had other weird things happening, like my appetite was gone, my gums were hurting when I brushed my teeth and I had some hair coming out. I started thinking I had MS or something else. I was FREAKING out!

After a couple doctors said I just had to wait it out and let my body adjust, I decided that wasn't an acceptable answer, as being this fatigued wasn't normal for me. I ended up going to a functional medicine doctor who diagnosed me with adrenal fatigue (that included a hormone imbalance of cortisol), two months after I had self-diagnosed myself with the same thing. I also found out I had an active Epstein Barr infection, which is the virus that causes mono. So that explained the insane fatigue and overall lack of energy. Basically, two years of chronic stress from fertility treatments had wiped my immune system out. I just had to figure out how to reset and heal.

Now that I'm eight months past ending fertility treatments, I can say that I don't at all regret trying to have a child, but I do kind of regret the shit I put into my body and what I did to my mental and physical health during the process. But once again, I'm battling through.

Sitting here finishing this book, I think back over the past two years and can honestly say that trying to have a baby artificially on my own was the hardest, most emotionally crazy part of my life. I look back at the money I spent (especially on donor sperm, ugh), the constant tears, the hormonal roller coaster (I apologize to all of my friends and family for THAT craziness ... well, and the ongoing hormonal craziness that has developed since) and the longing I had to raise a good little human in this struggling world we're all living in, and I really can't believe I went through all of it, let alone survived it. I truly didn't see how depressed I was during all of it. Getting pregnant so fast, having a miscarriage, going right back into treatment and procedures, over and over again. How I didn't end up in the looney bin from all of it, I'll never know.

Any experience I have, good or bad, I really do work to try to find the lesson in it. My biggest lesson from trying to have a baby? Well, it's that I am not in control of ANYTHING. After years of being manipulated in relationships, and men and various friends emotionally and physically abandoning me over and over again, I realized I started over-controlling my life — career, money, relationships, emotions — so I'd feel safe and protected from getting hurt. But I realize now that is no way to live. You see, you miss out on a lot of love and experiences when you put up such walls. Being vulnerable will always be hard for me, but trying to have a baby and struggling with getting pregnant broke me down like I had never been broken before, and finally made me be OK with the fact that I am NOT always strong, I am NOT always OK and sometimes things are HARD. I never used to allow myself to say things like that because I always wanted to be strong and resilient. Well, I realize now that part of being resilient is being able to say you're in a rough spot, and pushing through it. I know now, and will confidently say, that I am resilient as hell.

After I stopped treatments, there was zero doubt that I was done. I felt excited to get back to my life and have other hopes and dreams again. It was only after I stopped treatments, and while I was writing this book, that I had an epiphany and realized the ultimate lesson of my experience:

The past 24 years were a true journey to self worth. I didn't need a relationship or a man or a baby to feel worthy. I felt it, all on my own, for the first time in my life. I didn't need to keep trying to fit a relationship into my life, or a child, or defend to anyone why I was single, in order to feel worthy.

> I am enough all on my own.

I reject the notion that "something is wrong with me" if I'm not in a relationship or if I don't have children. I refuse to settle for someone who doesn't lift me up or enhance my life. I refuse to be in a relationship just because society says I should be, or settle and say, "Well, this is as good as it gets." Who wants to be on the receiving end of that? Not me. I also, as a woman, don't have to have a child to "feel like a woman" or feel complete. I am already complete.

The word "alone" is entirely different than how I'd describe my life. I don't feel alone. I have an amazing social network of friends, a close family with five nieces and nephews and some pretty awesome furbabies. I seek out new experiences and travel when I can. I have created myself and my life, and am not defined by a relationship or a child. I am my own person. And if that is what alone feels like, keep signing me up.

Now does this mean I won't ever be in a relationship again? Maybe. It depends. Now that I've found my worth and finally have standards, I know I will never, ever settle for someone who doesn't add something to my life, support me and bring a healthy love into my life. I am more protective over myself now, at age 44, than I ever have been, but I am open to receiving love if it's healthy.

And does this mean I've lost the desire to have a child? No, it doesn't. It just means I won't try artificial measures and inject myself with hormones again. I still have a lot of the baby feels and am trying to work through what that looks like for me. I may still be able to get pregnant naturally, if I'd happen to meet someone, or maybe I'll foster and adopt someday. I'm just trying to let it simmer and see where my heart and the universe take me. I decided trying to over control it was probably hindering the process, and sometimes you just have to sit back and know that the universe will bring things to your life that are meant to be there.

    I believe these experiences I've mentioned in this book were always meant to be part of my journey. My path has never been and will never be straight and has instead been filled with some pretty sharp detours with big mountains to climb that honestly seemed never ending at times. But I'm proud of how I've handled it all. Most of the time with my head up, but sometimes, with my head down. I honestly feel that I had to walk this path until I woke up. The universe kept presenting the same situation to me in a different guy and put me in tough situations (house, job, trying to have a baby on my own) until I got the lesson that I am capable of handling a lot of shit and having a happy life all on my own, not in a relationship, not depending on or defining myself by a man or by having a child. I had to learn to stop being codependent and stop basing my happiness on another person. That is too much pressure and expectation to put on another person, and it prevents you from finding true joy inside yourself and the world around you. My joy and my worth are all inside of ME.

It's been in front of me the entire time, all these years. I just had to see it.

The baby journey has made me more vulnerable, more kind and more open than I've ever been. I couldn't have gone through all this pain though and let it be in vain. Maybe my purpose was to experience all of the shit and share it. Maybe the universe was redirecting me to this all along. It's important to speak our truths and struggles so that maybe one other person will say "Yea, I went through that, too," and will feel a little less alone. Maybe that's part of what this entire journey has been about, using my struggles to help others.

I talked to my best friend, Marcia, on the phone the other day after she did a pre-read on this book. She said something that I had never even considered or realized while writing it. "Lauri, you say you 'failed' at singing, rafting, relationships, having a baby, but you didn't. Don't you see? All of it was for love! Love for yourself, love for life and love for others. You didn't fail at anything. You have LIVED."

Right then and there all the dots connected. My journey has truly been one of love. And it all led to me finally loving myself.

What has been the biggest lesson of your life?

Do you feel complete and happy on your own? What helped you achieve that?

If not, what can you do to love yourself more?

Acknowledgements

To my mom, thank you for loving me unconditionally and for your unwavering support always, especially during my fertility journey. I greatly appreciate you joining me on the long drives to and from Cleveland and for sharing in my hope. We had some early mornings (4 a.m.) — the four-hour trips went so much faster with our conversations! I'll always remember sharing a hotel room with you and the laughs we got out of that! I love you.

To my aunt Vickie, my sister Kerri, my brother Sean, Fred and the rest of my family and all of my incredible tribe of friends, thank you. Thank you for never judging me for trying to become a single mother by choice. Thank you for cheering me on every step of the way, celebrating my pregnancy with me and then crying with me when I lost it. I wouldn't have been able to get through those 1.5 years without every single one of you by my side. It means more to me than you will ever know.

To my friend Jennifer, thank you for designing the most beautiful cover for this book. You are an amazing, elegant and creative designer. You know me so well and captured my heart and the emotions perfectly. You also have been such a caring, supportive friend, and for that I am grateful. Thank you. Please visit Jennifer's website to check out all her designs at **http://www.jenrowedesign.com.**

To Debbie for editing the book, you rock woman! Your friendship has been unwavering. **And pre-readers Chad, Terra and Marcia,** thank you for being there for me and taking time to read my personal journey to provide me great, honest feedback and reviews. I love you all!

And finally, **to my angel baby,** who I lost the weekend of Jan. 12, 2018, thank you for making me a mom, even if it was only for eight weeks. I still think about you all the time even though I never got to hold you in my arms. You'll forever be in my heart.

About the Author

Lauri Tucker lives in Columbus, Ohio, with her cat fur babies Charlie and Mini, and works as a marketing communications professional. Lauri is passionate about helping others find their worth and living their most positive lives. She continuously works to grow and evolve, and reinvents herself each year through new goals and unique experiences. She pursues happiness daily by writing, working out, biking, hiking, kayaking, drinking wine and eating chocolate, and also by spending time with friends, family, and of course, her rescue cats. Paddling Upstream is her first book. She invites you to visit her online at **paddlingupstream.me.** Please share your feedback with her there and help promote the book online by using the hashtag #paddlingupstreambook.

www.ingramcontent.com/pod-product-compliance
Lightning Source LLC
Chambersburg PA
CBHW051405290426
44108CB00015B/2162